Vital Ministry in the Small-Membership Church
HEALTHY ESTEEM

Anthony G. Pappas

DISCIPLESHIP RESOURCES

P.O. BOX 340003 • NASHVILLE, TN 37203-0003
www.discipleshipresources.org

Cover and book design by Joey McNair

Edited by Linda R. Whited and David Whitworth

ISBN 0-88177-372-7

Scripture quotations, unless otherwise indicated, are from the New Revised Standard Version of the Bible, copyright © 1989 by the Division of Christian Education of the National Council of the Churches of Christ in the USA. All rights reserved. Used by permission.

HEALTHY ESTEEM. Copyright © 2002 Discipleship Resources. All rights reserved. No part of this book may be reproduced in any form whatsoever, print or electronic, without written permission, except in the case of brief quotations embodied in critical articles or reviews. For information regarding rights and permissions, contact Discipleship Resources, P.O. Box 340003, Nashville, TN 37203-0003; phone 800-814-7833 (toll-free) or 615-340-7068; fax 615-340-1789; e-mail mgregory@gbod.org.

DR372

Contents

Foreword 4

Esteem Issues 7

Esteem Onstage 15

Esteem Building 31

ABC's of Small-Church Esteem 35

Bibliography 37

Foreword

Mirror, Mirror, on the wall
Who is the fairest of us all?

These simple words spoken by the queen in the story *Snow White* to her magic mirror helped her discover her own beauty. Of course, she was beautiful, but unfortunately one day the mirror told her that Snow White was even fairer. Enraged by the claim, the queen jealously set out on a mission that would ultimately destroy her.

Churches can suffer from the "mirror complex" by gaining their value and worth from the opinions of others. Sometimes I hear leaders of small churches ask: "Are we a strong small church?" "Are we healthy enough?" "Should we be bigger?" "Should we be more faithful?" Sometimes church leaders may publicly claim "bigger is better, smaller is weaker, why aren't you more like . . . ," which reinforces a sense of poor, even unhealthy, self-esteem in small-church congregations.

The tragedy in believing what others tell you about yourself is that you may also be blinded to the truth about yourself. Rather than competing with other churches (who may be bigger, and so forth), small churches should claim their God-given strengths and respond to their own unique call to ministry and do it well. Sometimes this response means focusing on one thing your congregation does well that will make a difference in your community. Perhaps you can collaborate with another church or organization in your community and offer your strengths toward a success of shared ministry. Having a significant ministry begins with a winning attitude, not with whining. Significant ministry is grounded in a sense of abundance (what you have) rather than in a sense of scarcity (what you do not have).

Anyone can see *that* the small church is different from the megachurches. But it takes a wise person to see *how* the small church is different from the Willow Creeks or larger "First" churches.

Tony Pappas offers the small church a clever way to assess its own esteem. In this book he:

- defines esteem;
- reminds us that small, which is actually the church norm, can be effective in its mission;
- offers a creative murder mystery to challenge our values; and
- provides reflection questions and exercises for leaders to test the health of our own churches' esteem.

(Psst ... I'll give you a clue about the mystery: Basically, it's not about size—it's about spiritual significance!)

With joy,
Julia Kuhn Wallace, Director
Small Membership Church and Shared Ministry
General Board of Discipleship, Nashville, Tennessee

Esteem Issues

>Whether you think you can or whether you think you can't, either way you are right.[1]

For individuals, self-concept goes a long way in determining effectiveness in the world. A person with modest abilities but with a self-image of competence will often accomplish more than a person with greater competence who is insecure and filled with self-doubt. And the person with a sense of personal worth and security tends to be happier and more fulfilled than the person lacking these qualities. One's attitude toward one's self is a powerful indicator of productivity and joy in life.

This is no less true of churches. I am the Area Minister (a position comparable to that of district superintendent in The United Methodist Church) for fifty-two American Baptist congregations in southeastern Massachusetts. One of my churches I call "The Little Church That Could." They surveyed the community and found that to most people they were invisible. So they held a series of Christian rock concerts on their front lawn. That got folk's attention! They also realized that preschool care and teaching was needed in their community, so they started their own daycare ministry. Though not particularly large in membership, they have sent two laypersons out to other congregations to bolster Christ's ministry in those locations. They pull off hands-on mission trips and exciting social events. Whatever they think God would have them do, they start; and because they believe it will happen, it does.

Another one of my churches closed recently. At the time of the closing they had a serviceable building in good repair and over $150,000 in the bank! But they did not believe they could accomplish anything more. "Nothing we have done has worked," they told me. At the meeting to vote on closing, there emerged a number of new things to try. But their self-attitude prevented them from choosing anything but closure.

The sum of all of these attitudes toward one's self we label "self-esteem." Healthy, or high, self-esteem allows people and congregations to function productively and joyously. Unhealthy, or low, self-esteem robs people and churches of happiness and effectiveness. Small churches are particularly vulnerable to low self-esteem. The onus is not entirely on the local congregation, though, for we live in an environment that is not conducive to high congregational esteem. Consider these factors:

> … we live in an environment that is not conducive to high congregational esteem.

1. **Societal Values.** The dominant culture in the United States values bigness. Being large and growing rapidly are where it is at. Smallness is perceived as a form of failure. Though the Bible offers an alternative value framework, it is difficult to avoid society's prescription.
2. **Discouraging Trends.** Most small churches are not just small; they are also smaller and weaker and older and more disheartened than they were even ten years ago. It is hard to feel good about one's self when memory mocks.
3. **Changing Environment.** A century ago if the self-esteem of a small church was ebbing, the congregation could choose to buck up, have a revival, reconnect with its social context, see God reward its efforts, and begin to feel good again. Today the average small church doesn't

have a clue about how to relate to its environment, no matter how repentant and "revivaled" they become. The people around the church know little about Christianity, likely speak a different language, and certainly have a different worldview.[2] It is hard to feel powerful in the face of impotency!

Although these factors are significant and will not magically go away, they need not be the primary factors affecting esteem in the small church. Consider four reasons why each and every small church can experience rising levels of self-esteem.

1. *It is not about you anyway.* Church, large or small, is about the power of God to enter into and transform human experience. It is about God. God is the actor whose presence really matters in each congregation. When, like Peter, we shift our eyes off of Jesus and onto the waves that assail us, we start to sink (Matthew 14:22-33). We are important because the spirit of the living God chooses to indwell the social form we call our church. The Apostle Paul reminds us that we are guardians of spiritual treasures in earthen vessels (2 Corinthians 4:5-7). This fundamental truth is not an excuse to be small in our thinking, weak in our faith, dysfunctional in our operations, conflicted in our relations, limited in our fruitfulness, and paralyzed in our old patterns. But it is a reason to remember that the power we proclaim is first, last, and always God's power and not ours.

2. *The small congregation is the normative form of the body of Christ across the globe, across twenty centuries!* In the first three centuries following Christ's birth, congregations were almost exclusively house churches. Seldom

> Church, large or small, is about the power of God to enter into and transform human experience.

did they have even as many as thirty members.³ Yet the Christian faith spread like wildfire until it came to dominate the Roman Empire. The small congregation is the first, powerful, and standard form of the church. Why is this so hard to grasp? In contemporary Christianity it is hard to see because our vision is blocked.

I speak to many gatherings of small-church leaders each year. Often I will raise self-esteem issues by asking this question: Something of significance for small churches happened in A.D. 33, in the late 1800's, and in 1965; what were these happenings? Usually groups can figure out what the first date signifies: the resurrection of Jesus Christ. (Although groups that say only, "Jesus died," make me wonder about their belief in a living God!) I then get some wild answers for the next two dates. What I am after, I explain, is the fact that the late 1800's marked the beginning of the construction of public transit systems in major urban areas.⁴ So for the first time in human history, thousands of people could get to a one- or two-hour event and get home for lunch! So large churches, big steeples, big pulpits, Old Firsts came into being. As we think of them today, large churches have only been around for a little over a century—only 5% of the history of our faith. They are but a recent blip on the radar screen. Though small churches tend to live in the shadow of these large churches and their megachurch offspring, our rightful historical place is in the center of God's salvation drama.

1965? The largest percentage of Americans attended worship in 1965. The proportion rose until it peaked in 1965, and it has receded dramatically since that year.⁵ What this means for small-church people is that a large number of the

> The small congregation is the first, powerful, and standard form of the church.

members can remember a day when their current small church was a mid-sized church or at least a robust small congregation. With this memory comes a great sense of grief and loss. So it is that small-church people can't find their place in the sun. They think they are in the shadow of the large church. Or if not, they whimper in their own shadow, the shadow of what used to be.

This sense of grief and loss is a great shame. For the fact of the matter is that the small congregation is the normative form of the body of Christ across the globe, across twenty centuries!

3. *There is a Divine genius about the small church.* The Bible tells us that human beings were made in the image of the divine. Though we individually fall short, that fact is the truth about our being. Just so, the small church is redemptive in its natural functioning. The natural processes of life in a healthy small congregation reflect God's intention for humanity. When it gathers, the small church has the quality and feel of a family reunion. Have you ever tried to silence the folk as they enter the sanctuary of a small church? Good luck! They are spontaneously celebrating their bonds of love. In this natural process each is affirmed, each one's place acknowledged, each one's meaning confirmed. It is heaven without the harps. From this love, joy arises. "I was glad when they said to me, 'Let us go to the house of the LORD' " (Psalm 122:1). It is blessed to be with loved ones, bask in God's presence, banter and tease. Warmth in the heart and a smile on the lips are the consequences of the healthy small church gathered.

But, conversely, there is no place to hide in the small congregation. If you are being stupid, selfish, unspiritual, pig-headed, or pouty, you

> The natural processes of life in a healthy small congregation reflect God's intention for humanity.

can't hide in the small church. In the reality of face-to-face relationships, one can't "niche out," stay in one's comfort zone, and so avoid growth-demanding experiences.

By its nature, the small church needs everyone's involvement. There are plenty of opportunities to serve, to try out new skills, or to plug a gap. The small church is one big standing invitation to low-threat, high-affirmation experiences.

One Sunday an organist in a small-membership church had one of her preteen students play the offertory on the piano. The student apparently hadn't learned that the repeat in a score is meant to be done only once! The whole congregation was treated to ten minutes of interesting, but highly repetitive, music. Finally, she finished, but the delight in remembering that effort will go on forever. That foible was a small price to pay for the affirmation of each and every contribution!

Also, in the small church, behavioral change is often effected through acculturation. People become more Christlike by catching it from those who are a bit farther down the road. Acculturation can have a downside, too, but it is easier, more fun and natural, and often longer lasting than changes accomplished by force of will. Furthermore ... well, you get the idea.

4. *Small churches, on average, are more effective in evangelism and have more quality of Christian faithfulness.* This is an amazing statement. I do not have the chutzpah to make it, but I am delighted to quote it and pass it along to you. Christian Schwarz, a congregational consultant and researcher, has administered an instrument of 170 items to over a thousand churches in thirty-two countries. As he sifted through this mountain of data, he found that

> The small church is one big standing invitation to low-threat, high-affirmation experiences.

small churches grow, on average, at a 13% rate and large churches at 3%! Also, small churches have a four-point advantage in his quality rating, and the three factors that correlate most negatively with church growth are liberal theology, traditionalism, and large church size! Read all about it in *Natural Church Development*. Schwarz concludes that "the evangelistic effectiveness of minichurches [churches with less than one hundred worshipers] is statistically 1,600 percent greater than that of megachurches."[6]

Small church. High self-esteem. You may have considered these two phrases mutually exclusive. Time to reconsider. Small churches are the divinely constructed form for service on earth, and they are a foretaste of heaven, too! The small church that has a positive self-understanding will be used mightily of God. The small church that feels defeated takes itself out of the game and grieves God's heart.

Now if your church is a small church with low levels of self-esteem, don't get depressed about it. You can change and emerge into God's joyous intention. The first step is to start enjoying life in the small lane. The next section of this booklet is designed to put a smile on your face as you learn more about the unique advantages of the small congregation.

> The small church that has a positive self-understanding will be used mightily of God.

Endnotes

1 Some attribute this quotation to Henry Ford, a few to Abraham Lincoln, some to Thomas Edison. Whoever said it, it makes a point.

2 See *Death of the Church*, by Mike Regele (Zondervan Publishing House, 1995), especially chapters 10 through 12.

3 See *Paul's Idea of Community: The Early House Churches in Their Historical Setting,* by Robert Banks (William B. Eerdmans Publishing Company, 1980), pages 40-42.

4 Note, for example, the effect of "Beecher's boats," as described in *Ben Franklin's Web Site: Privacy and Curiosity from Plymouth Rock to the Internet,* by Robert Ellis Smith (Privacy Journal, 2000), page 214.

5 See "Americans Running Low on 'Social Capital,'" article in the *Providence Journal,* November 13, 1999.

6 From *Natural Church Development: A Guide to Eight Essential Qualities of Healthy Churches,* by Christian A. Schwarz (ChurchSmart Resources, 1996), pages 46-48.

Esteem Onstage

Welcome to what I trust will be an enjoyable way to enter into deeper understandings about the nature of the small church. The play you are about to read did not really happen, except in my imagination. None of the characters resemble any person living or dead—no matter how much you may think so!

When you perform this play, the audience is permitted to laugh, so please instruct the actors that only the corpse need have a grimace on his or her face! If folks insist on being serious, they may do so during the discussion time, when they will be required to answer the questions provided, since their eternal destiny may hinge on their responses!

Tips on Stage Managing This Reading Play

I have spontaneously sprung this play any number of times on groups of up to one hundred. I usually ask for audience volunteers, such as thespian wannabes, people in Shy Persons Anonymous, and/or Extrovert Addicts. Note that any of the nine parts may be read by either women or men, giving proper attention to the *he*'s and *she*'s and to some of the characters' names.

Also take note of these other points:
- The organizer of the play should take the Narrator role.
- Most of the acting instructions are included with the lines.
- If possible, let the actors read through the play once or twice to get a sense of their parts. Some of the lines are deliberately cumbersome, and so a chance to practice hamming it up is helpful.
- The Narrator's lines sometimes describe the physical movements

of the actors, allowing them to simply do what is being read about them.
- Write the name of each character on a sign to hang around the actor's neck.
- Suggested discussion questions and some tips on the process are found at the end of the play.

Enjoy. Have fun. Learn a bit. And blessings on your life of faithfulness in your small church.

The Great Small-Church Conference Preparation Meeting Murder Mystery

Characters

Narrator
Welton Kumb
  (known as Wel Kumb)
Rev. Woodrow B. True
  (known as Woodie)
Bishop R. U. Biggeryet
Rev. D. Godwrath
Karl Kuddly
Parish Sage
Rabid Day
Rev. Ulysses Didditt

Narrator: Rev. Woodrow B. True—known as Woodie—smiled as he tied the small skiff to the dock. He was pleased and excited. He, the man had said, had been selected from all of the hundreds of thousands of small-church pastors across the globe to host the first annual Small, Local, International Council of Churches—the SLICC—because, the man had continued, of the wonderful job he was doing as pastor in his small, coastal congregation (*pause*) and because of the fine retreat house the church had been bequeathed last year. Woodie paused on the dock to look up at the retreat house. Covering almost all of the tiny island, a five-minute putt-putt journey from the town dock, it appeared fortress solid. The granite had been imported in a more prosperous day to form its walls, which rose almost sheer from the water. Little did Woodie suspect that by nightfall the joy of the moment would be shattered.

Wel: Hallo, Woodie. If I had known how much advance work there is to retreats, I'd have never taken this job as ... uh, ministry ... as High-and-Dry Retreat House Director. When you said I would be handling the arrangements for small-church retreats, I thought you meant *small* church retreats! You know, like five or six people. Why, there are over a hundred people signed up for tomorrow's retreat. And now you spring on me that all these bigwigs are coming early!

Woodie: OK, OK. So we'll pay you overtime, Welton. But the response to the conference is encouraging, isn't it? That's why the leadership team decided to meet a day ahead. You know, to make sure we are all coordinated, to get things ready, to go over the flow. Bigger numbers mean more administration, more planning, less spontaneity, less responsiveness.

Wel: I'd rather go with the flow. But don't worry, the library will be all ready for them by mid-afternoon.

Narrator: Wel Kumb was as good as his word. Having ferried the luminaries—who, he determined, could not walk on water—over on perfectly calm, too calm, waters, he deposited their respective bags in their respective rooms. Wel was now serving coffee as each of them arrived in the library at three o'clock. Finishing that task, he announced that a nor'easter was a-brewing and that if they lacked anything he would do his best to obtain it, but not to count on it. It was only a moment later when they heard the sound of his skiff's outboard, at full throttle, heading for the mainland. The small-church-conference leaders gathered 'round the circular table. They introduced themselves—mostly for Woodie's benefit—and shared the gist of their presentations.

Bishop: I am Bishop R. U. Biggeryet. I serve as Archbishop of Megalomania of the church of the Everbrighter Gospel Light. When I became bishop ten years ago, we had hundreds of small churches in my area. Through my unswerving efforts we have reduced that number to a mere score. Father Ulysses Didditt, who is also here (*the bishop points to a wizened man at the opposite end of the table*) to lead a workshop on survival—"Life Raft Techniques," I think he's dubbed it—can attest to this major movement forward. Through mandatory clergy retraining courses, a program to disenfranchise anti-progressive laypeople, mandated mergers, and the closing of redundant churches, we have virtually solved the small-church problem. I am prepared to share in great detail how all church hierarchies can adapt my techniques and achieve this final solution to the small-church problem.

Don: Thank you—I think—Bishop. My name is Rev. Godwrath. I have been a part of small churches all my life and have spent the last

Vital Ministry in the Small-Membership Church

decades systematically studying them. My research indicates that the small church as we have known it—a stable, culture-bearing community of faith, rooted in its open country, small village, or ethnic neighborhood environment, infectiously communicating the Christian faith to successive generations, and connected to its greater social, economic, and political community by engaging in ministries through natural relationship—this small church is almost extinct. It is certainly an endangered species! My address will give small-church people the courage to change the things that can be changed back, the serenity to accept the things that can't be changed back, and the wisdom to know the difference.

Karl: Umm, I was thinking, Don, as you were talking about those old-fashioned churches, that old single cell of caring people? —By the way, I'm Karl Kuddly. You've undoubtedly heard of my six-week program, "Making the Small Church More Kuddly." I designed it so that the small church could get back in touch with its nature. And, you ask, what is its nature? Well, its nature is to know and to be known—personally, I mean. In the small church everybody knows or knows about everybody else. Some are known intimately; some aren't; but everyone can be placed. This knowing is human and humanizing. I know the characters might fight with the doers, and the God-woman pray for them all, especially the pastor, but this structure of knowing and being known is how God intended it.

Parish Sage: Am I, Parish Sage, the only one who can see that you are all missing the point? Or to be more precise the 351 points? The small church is not one church, or one type of church, but an amazing succession of social forms kaleidoscoping upward in a centrifugal display of multiplicity, pluralism, and dysfunctionality. As I wrote so clearly and exhaustively in bulletin #7284...or was it book #518?... well, leaders in small churches must recognize which type of church theirs is if there is to be any hope for a successful ministry. Now the smallest small church is like a raccoon. It has hands like a human and so can get itself into, and occasionally out of, some pretty touchy situations. It has eyes like a bandit and sometimes steals the heart of an up-and-coming pastor. However, it seems to have trouble distinguishing between garbage and good stuff. Sometimes the denomination's menu of offerings is ignored, and one little tidbit is the only thing taken amidst loud complaints of malnourishment. And sometimes it just scatters lots of garbage everywhere. Now the next-sized church is like a wood stove. You may need to cut your own wood and stoke it up, sometimes even strike the match, but when it gets going, you can enjoy many hours of warmth. The next-sized small church is like a wheel. It has a hub, spokes, and a tire. It goes round and round. The hub thinks it is extremely busy, the spokes like the breeze blowing in their faces, and the tire is sometimes extremely tired. And if there is enough tread and enough spokes, they can get somewhere. Other-sized churches are like the chicken that crossed the road, the ancient Persian mail system, and the aurora borealis in its pre-nova phase.

Narrator: The silence that followed Parish Sage's speech was marred only by Woodie's under-the-breath comment that, simple though they were, the biblical images of the Body of Christ and the People of God still made a lot of sense to him.

Rabid Day: I'm Rabid Day. All this analysis is good, but what we really need is action. The small church will never get anywhere waiting for their denomination or the large churches or the seminaries to throw them a bone. They have to stand up and assert themselves to gain what is rightfully theirs. Well over half the mainline churches in our nation are small churches. Smaller churches have a rate of growth more than four times as fast as large churches. Small churches win at least as many new converts as large churches. In fact, a great strategy for evangelism would be to break larger churches up into smaller churches, since small churches are sixteen times more effective at evangelism than churches with over one thousand in attendance! Small churches have almost twice the proportion of people utilizing their spiritual gifts that megachurches do. And in small churches the percentage of people involved in small-group faith development is nearly four times larger than it is in megachurches.[1] They need to learn their denominational ropes and lobby for their rights. Why look at those *(Read the following statement or add information about the accomplishments of your own denomination.)*

United Methodists and American Baptists. The people in their small churches started talking to people, proposing that small churches should get as much attention as large churches, making their needs known. Now The United Methodist Publishing House has children's curriculum for small churches called *The One Room Sunday School*—which is doing quite well, by the way. And the American Baptists are recommending the *One Room Sunday School* materials for small churches and selling it through their own denominational catalog.

They are on the map. Assert. Act. Accomplish. That's what small churches need to do and that's what my workshop is about! Amen.

Narrator: Nobody wanted to argue with Rabid. Rev. Didditt didn't even know if he should speak up at all. Finally, after the bishop fixed his gaze upon him, he did.

Ulysses: Well, my name is Ulysses. I've served small churches in the same district for twenty years. I went where no one else wanted to go, way out in the boonies, far from civilization and the bishopric. It was under those circumstances that I learned a lot about survival—how you need to do whatever it takes and not just snap your fingers once for things to fall into place. Sometimes I had to work a job or two in addition to pastoring to make sure there was food on the table. Putting together a way for the church to survive always involved more than one source of support: tithing, pledging, bequests, memorials, special fundraisers, asking the bishop's office for help, and so forth. You do as much as it takes to get it done, and you're never satisfied that any one effort is enough. I guess I've learned my lessons well, because even though, as the bishop has said, the number of small churches in our area is shrinking, I will be taking on a new assignment in one of our smallest churches when I get back from this conference. (*Rev. Didditt sighs sadly.*)

Narrator: Amid congratulations and condolences offered to Ulysses by the others, the meeting broke up and each of the respective leaders adjourned to his or her respective room to rest before dinner. An hour later the group began assembling in the dining room. Parish

Sage sat in a Captain's chair and speculated aloud about the menu. Rabid hoped the meal was of a caloric level in proportion to third-world standards. Ulysses stood with his thumbs tucked into the elasticized waistband of his sports slacks.

Ulysses (*drawing a long breath*): I'm sure this conference will be a refreshing experience.

Karl: If it's a breath of fresh air you want, just open the door. It looks like a full-fledged gale out there to me.

Woodie: It's just a little nor'easter.

Narrator: Though they had been cut off from the mainland since Wel had wisely abandoned the island, it was certainly a temporary situation.

Woodie: Why, tomorrow the sun will shine as brightly as Ulysses' suspenders.

Narrator: All eyes focused on Ulysses' aforementioned article of apparel and squinted. Heads then turned, mumbling in chorus something about "hope springing."

Don: When I'm hungry, as I now am, I know my name—Godwrath—fits me perfectly. Are we all here now?

Woodie: The bishop's missing. I'll go fetch him.

(*Woodie exits and reappears a moment later on the landing.*)

Woodie: R. U.'s dead!

Karl: No. We's not. I know we're not too lively, but we'll pick up after a good supper.

Woodie (*with a note of urgency*): No. No. R. U. Biggeryet—the bishop—is dead!

Karl: Oh. Well, why didn't you say so?

(*All rush to the door of the bishop's room.*)

Ulysses: Are you sure he's dead?

Woodie: Of course; he's been shot!

Narrator: ...and stabbed...

Don: ...and poisoned...

Parish Sage: ...and bludgeoned...

Rabid Day: ...and strangled...

Narrator: Incredulous, Ulysses wiggled his way to the front of the group, peering in the doorway to see for himself.

Ulysses: It looks pretty definite. (*He sighs.*)

Narrator: Woodie, who had been pushed into the room by the throng, was again feeling like the host and took it upon himself to start investigating.

Woodie: Let me borrow your belt, Ulysses.

Narrator: Using the yard of leather as a loop, Woodie succeeded in confirming the most bizarre murder in small-church-conference history. Pulling the bishop's body slightly forward revealed clearly the dagger sunk to its hilt in his back. Easing the bishop's head back exposed a burning, red welt around the bishop's neck. The foam on the corpse's lips and the grimace on his face indicated a fast-acting poison. The blood-soaked depression on the top of his head matched exactly the fireplace poker not two feet away. Slowly pulling the bishop's body back onto the dagger's hilt revealed the powder burns where a small-caliber bullet had entered the heart.

Woodie: I don't get it. He's dead five times over. Whoever did it is most thorough and most vicious.

Narrator: Then it hit him! Maybe they all hated him. The man was hardly lovable. Maybe he could make you be pleasant to him, but he couldn't make you like it. Maybe they'd all had enough, and they had joined together, each in his own way, to send the bishop to his eternal reward up here while Woodie was downstairs warming the white sauce. What a thought! Enough to make you lose your appetite for white sauce for a while.

Karl: Who would have done such a thing? Whoever did it held no warm fuzzies in *his* heart or … (*looking around at the others*) in *her* heart.

Parish Sage: Well, it could have been any one of us. We were all up here resting and refreshing for an hour before dinner. Any one of us could have slipped in and done it.

All (*one after another*): Not me!

Parish Sage: Only Woodie is off the hook because he was downstairs readying the meal. My room is at the head of the stairs and I would have seen him. My door was open to better hear the call to dinner, which I would remind you has yet to come. (*He looks at Woodie reproachfully.*)

Rabid Day: Parish Sage, we've proved now that you don't know everything. There is a back staircase that leads directly from the kitchen to the landing by the bishop's door. So Woodie could have done it after all. (*Rabid smiles.*)

Parish Sage: Well, then, only the extent of the meal preparations can exonerate Woodie. I will go investigate.

Narrator: Parish Sage leaves, licking his lips and ignoring the accusation of fallibility.

Don: Let's call the police.

(All eyes shift to Woodie.)

Woodie: Great idea except for three things. One, in this storm all the phone lines are down.

Don: And two?

Woodie: And two, we don't have a phone here anyway. We handle all the retreat business at the church.

Don: And three?

Woodie: And three, we don't have a police department. It was voted out at last year's town meeting when it became known that we hadn't had a crime in five years.

Karl (*with hope*)**:** Well, now we have a crime, and that will lead to reinstating the police department, which will make all your parishioners feel a lot safer.

Narrator: It was at that point that Woodie started to erase Karl from his list of suspects.

Don: Parish Sage is eating and not present to defend the theory that it could have been any one of *us*, but I think it *could* have been someone else. Someone who snuck in whilst we were distracted. Maybe Wel or someone on a passing fishing boat or an unhinged church-growth activist.

Karl: Couldn't be. We all heard Wel motor away. We could see the dock from the library, and no one came or went after Wel. The walls are too steep and the rocks too slippery to allow access anywhere except at the dock. And anyone trying to enter the retreat house after our meeting in the library broke up would have let all kinds of wind and water in. And there isn't any.

Narrator: The clarity of Karl's reasoning led Rev. True to put him back on the list of suspects.

Woodie: Bravo. My logic exactly. One or more of us is the killer.

Narrator: The meeting in the library was not attended by happy people. The storm had severed the electrical line to the island. The stone building had been unwisely built sans fireplace, and the tiny gas heater did little to dispel the chill in the air. And in the flicker of candlelight the protestations of innocence seemed mocking and macabre. Rev. True asked each to explain why the rest should consider him innocent. They started with Karl and proceeded around the room, ending with Woodie.

Karl: I have been a small-church person all my life, and we small-church people know that death is not a solution. The fellowship of a small church has a certain shape. This shape has been molded over time, and although the shape is embodied by particular people, it transcends their individuality. It has become a function of the dynamic of the group. The group needs to function in a certain manner and elects someone to live it out. But when that person dies, the need of the group has not changed and so someone else takes over the antagonizing behavior. Every small-church pastor who has stayed long enough to bury someone knows what I am talking about. The thorn-in-the-side dies, and the pastor breathes a sigh of relief for exactly five minutes, and then the group contorts. And someone new becomes Mr. Thorn-in-the-Side. Maybe over the same issue. Maybe over something else—just to keep the pastor humble. Hopes come crashing down. Death is not the answer. Only slow and patient transformation toward health by the working of the Spirit is. No small-church person would ever think that death, let alone murder, ever solved anything. So if I had hated R. U., which I assure you I did not, I would not have thought to kill him. On the contrary, I would have liked to keep him alive so I could harass the living daylights out of him!

Narrator: "Whew, the prickly side of Kuddly," thought Woodie.

Vital Ministry in the Small-Membership Church

Don: The small church nourishes my spirit and has for many a year. I minister in Christ's name, along with the others in my small church, as we work to relieve some of the inequities in our little town. We have such hopes, and we give it our best effort, but we know that God gives the increase. And you know how we know? Because our resources are never adequate to the task. When we wanted to rebuild widow Smith's house after it was gutted by fire, we had no idea where the material was going to come from. Or for that matter, the skilled labor either. But we started in faith. And word got out. And somebody dropped off some sheetrock. And an electrician heard about it and gave the project a day of his time for nothing. Miracle after little miracle occurred, and we finished the house for Mrs. Smith. Well, really, God did.

Karl (*puzzled*): So, that means you're innocent?

Don: Sure. No small-church person would bring poison, a gun, a knife, and a poker to do a job. That's too many resources. That is not living at the margin, where God has called us.

Karl (*scratching his head*): Well, I guess you can't argue with that.

Woodie: Parish Sage, what do you have to say?

Parish Sage: Well, I can tell you one thing for sure: the person who did this was not a small-church person. Although there may be a bit of hope in a large-church ministry—after doing the time, of course. The reason for this conclusion can be stated in one word: planning. Small-church people don't plan much. That is, they don't plan to do new and different things. Of course, it is technically possible that if the killer is a serial killer, he could be a small-church person, but that seems unlikely. Small-church people plan to do what they did at this time last year, or they might do something on the spur of the moment. But for sure they wouldn't plan to the extent that this killer did: bringing along a knife, a gun, a poker, and poison. And maybe a rope, too. No, this was not done by a small-church person. And in my heart I have always been a wood-stove kind of person!

Rabid Day: Everyone knows my commitment to the small church, and how small-church I am in my essence, and how much time and energy I have put into getting small-church people to work together to change the system. Therefore, you know I didn't do it, because if I had done it, it wouldn't be a private thing. I would have had a covered-dish supper first. Then we would have had a formal business meeting. Then we would have adjourned out to the parking lot, where we would figure out what we really felt about bumping off this guy. Then we would have gone and done it together, noted the date, so that we could commemorate it every year, and made a big tradition out of it. You know, like the "We Killed the Bishop Pancake Breakfast," $4.50 for adults. See, I didn't do it. It wasn't my style!

Woodie (*turning quickly to face Ulysses*)**:** But it was your style, wasn't it, Rev. U. Didditt! It is just your style to overdo whatever you do. I first started wondering about you when I noticed you were wearing elasticized trousers, a belt, and suspenders! That is most unusual to say the least. But it was your approach to life to distrust any one thing, to overact, to overcompensate. You told us that was how you learned to survive in your congregation. And that was how you approached this murder, too. You overprepared, bringing five different means of death along with you. And you overacted, using all five to make sure his bishopness died.

Ulysses: No. No. No. You've got it wrong. Yes, I used five means of death because I really wanted him dead, but I brought ten means along with me. I was determined not to fail.

Woodie: He thought you were a failure, and you were going to show him?

Ulysses: Oh, no! He knew I was a success, and he was determined to break me. Twenty years ago I was assigned a struggling little church a thousand miles away from the bishop. I enjoyed the independence and soon found that the church was growing by leaps and bounds. Soon it began to dawn on me that I could have a problem. If the bishop thought that my church was "significant," I could start to expect more interference. Maybe even reassignment if I appeared uncooperative. So I "adjusted" the annual reports to his office to keep the appearance of a small, struggling church. After all, even if the bishop decided to visit every parish in the conference, it would be retirement time before he got around to me. And for nearly two decades, it worked fine. I had a big, bustling church with plenty of programs, lots of planning for the future, lots of left-brain activity, and a big salary. And, because he thought we were too small to bother with, no bother from the bishop. But something happened last year, and R. U. started asking some awkward questions. Then I knew it. He was on to me. He was transferring me to a really small, struggling situation, but by this time I was hooked on bigness. The thought of such a change drove me into a rage. Then the invitation to this conference arrived. The plan to solve this problem once and for all emerged in my mind. And I came so close to succeeding. If only I could have slipped it by Rev. Woodie B. True. (*Didditt buries his head in his hands and starts sobbing.*)

Parish Sage: What a fool. Imagine being a large-church pastor and hiding it under a bushel! Incomprehensible.

Karl: Imagine taking a human life.

Wel: Bah! It was only a bishop.

Woodie: Wel! When did you get here?

Wel: The storm's let up. It's going to be a glorious day tomorrow, small-church folks!

The End

Endnote

1 This data is taken from *Natural Church Development: A Guide to Eight Essential Qualities of Healthy Churches,* by Christian A. Schwarz (ChurchSmart Resources, 1996), pages 46-48.

Discussion

If your group consists of fewer than twenty-five people, you may want to work as one group and record comments on newsprint. If the group numbers twenty-five or more, break into subgroups of six to eight. Appoint a scribe for each group. If time is limited, select only the questions that are most important for your group.

- What thoughts or feelings did you experience during this play?
- What elements of the play were true to your small-church experience? Which did not ring true?
- What did you learn about the nature of small churches through this play? What was missing?
- The play pokes some fun at bigness. What are your feelings and theology about big churches as compared with your small church?
- How do you feel about your small church's relationship with your denomination? What would make this relationship more fruitful?
- Is your small church stuck in the past? If so, did the play offer any insight for moving forward?
- A number of church gurus have labeled the small church an endangered species. What options lie ahead for small churches? For yours in particular?
- Are your church's leaders aware of congregational-size-dynamics analysis? (See the bibliography section for reading suggestions.)
- What ways can you envision for small churches to further their sense of potency and self-esteem?
- What steps can your congregation take to further its corporate health and make its internal relationships more loving? Are there particular patterns that impede love and health?
- How does your congregation deal with the fact of limited resources? Can you be faithful and bold in the face of insufficiency?
- What are the planning patterns in your church? Do they work? Are you missing opportunities for service and growth by working only out of a traditional planning pattern?
- Is your small church filled with joy? Are you able to celebrate the specialness of being small? How can abundant joy be released within your small church?
- Tell a fun story (hopefully not about a murder!) from your church's past.

Esteem Building

The following exercises may be done in study or fellowship groups or in conjunction with covered-dish suppers, desserts, and so forth. They can be done at one sitting, but I would recommend one a month in order to reinforce the movement toward more positive self-esteem.[1]

Exercise Number 1: *Doings!*

- Provide plenty of newsprint and markers.
- Appoint two scribes to share the duties of writing on newsprint.
- Have the whole group call out all of the things that have gone on in and through the church over the past year. These may be just listed as named or they may be formatted. (For example, see if the group can name an activity for each letter of the alphabet. Spelling variants are allowed! My church spelled *ecumenical* as 'Qumenical'!)
- After the list is complete, review it and

    ☺ Put a smiley face next to the activities the members enjoyed most.

    ♥ Put a heart next to the activities which provide entry points for new people.

    ★ Put a star next to the activities which the group desires to undergird and expand in the upcoming year.

    ✔ Put a check mark next to the activities which most closely reflect the congregation's nature and personality.

- Ask "What have we learned about ourselves from this exercise?"

Exercise Number 2: *The Badge of Honor*

- Form into groups of up to six people.

- Have newsprint and crayons for each group.

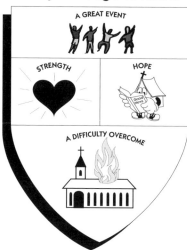

Sample "Badge of Honor"

- Have each group draw a Badge of Honor with four sections. Tell them to discuss each of the four topics and then draw in the appropriate section of the badge a picture or symbol that represents the consensus of their group. Here are the topics:
  1. a great event in the church's past
  2. a current strength of the congregation
  3. a hope the congregation holds for its future
  4. a difficulty that the church overcame in the past.

- When every group has finished, let each group show their badge and explain its meaning to the whole group.

- A new group may be formed to capture the recurrent answers in a new and artistic Badge of Honor for the whole congregation.

- Display the individual group badges and/or the total-group badge in a place where people can see the badges as they arrive for worship. Include a list of the questions that were used to determine what pictures and symbols would appear on the badges.

Exercise Number 3: *An Old Friend*

- Form into groups of up to six people.
- Have a notepad and pen ready for each group.
- Appoint a scribe for each group.
- Have each group write a letter to a distant relative describing your congregation as "an old friend."

  Some Things to Consider Mentioning
  Gender
  Age
  Ethnicity
  Preferences in Food, Dress, Activities
  Hobbies
  Appearance
  Personality type
  Quirks
  Strengths
  Weaknesses
  Maturity
  History
  The Nature of the Friendship: demanding, caring, possessive, supportive, fun-loving, and so forth

- Each group can share its description with the whole body.
- Volunteers may synthesize the descriptions into one to be printed in the church's newsletter or hung on the wall.

Exercise Number 4: *Pastors and Teams*

- Provide newsprint and markers.
- List all the previous pastors of the church that the group can remember.
- By discussion, decide which three (or two or four) pastors had the most fruitful ministry in your church.
- Break into three (or two or four) subgroups, one for each pastor.
- Let each group address these questions and record their wisdom about the pastor they were assigned.
    1. What made this ministry fruitful?
    2. What were the particular gifts of that pastor?
    3. How did the congregation "team" with that pastor to build a fruitful ministry?
    4. What does this say about the kind of leadership we prefer?
    5. What does this say about how we function and work together?
- Report each group's findings to the whole body. For each group's report, ask: What areas of rejoicing are indicated? What areas for further growth are indicated? How can the congregation celebrate or learn in the days ahead?

Endnote

1 Similar exercises of this type may be found in *Entering the World of the Small Church,* by Anthony G. Pappas (Alban Institute, 2000), pages 99-101.

ABC's of Small-Church Esteem

The pastor could barely wait for the speaker to ask for questions. He bolted to his feet and waved his arms to be recognized. The folk gathered at the annual small-church conference craned their necks to see what was so important.

The pastor addressed the speaker: "When you spoke at our conference three years ago, you said one thing that stuck with me. You said, 'Don't try to be another-sized church. God has a purpose for you at this time as a small church. Rather try to be the best small church you can be.' I chewed on that awhile and came to believe it. So I relaxed about what we weren't doing and started to enjoy what we were doing! I started to have fun in the ministry again. After a bit the church leaders wondered what I was up to, so I told them of my new perspective. In time they saw things that way too. Then that attitude started to permeate the congregation as a whole. We saw ourselves in a new light. Joy returned! We started to value ourselves as God's instrument right here, right now. And our numbers picked up a bit. But more importantly, we are feeling good about being faithful!"

Hopefully, by now you are seeing your small church as worthy in God's eyes, as having a special task to accomplish, as having a special place in God's scheme of things. But how can you reinforce these insights in the rest of your congregation and keep esteem healthy? Well, here are some ABC's:

A is for Admit. Admit it when your congregation does something well. Too often we look for the bad and then assign blame. How about if we took the time to acknowledge the good that God is doing through us? Accentuate the positive!

B is for Bunch. Keep your eyes open for multiple positives that occur in a short time frame. Three or more things to celebrate when bunched together can have the effect of changing the congregation's self-perception! Bunching can give a congregation's esteem a quantum boost!

C is for Celebrate. Praise God; thank one another; affirm each other's efforts and accomplishments. Have a party. Dance a jig. Sing a song! Have you ever seen high school athletes after a win? They hug and jump and yell and pig-pile. Aren't the victories of eternity worthy of even greater celebration?

D is for Dare. Dare to do even more for the Lord. Dare to become even more for the Lord. Congregations that rise to a challenge—whether or not they succeed—come to view themselves as players!

A+B+C+D= E

E is for Esteem. God is doing a great thing. Believe that God can do great things in and through your small church, and it will happen! God has called you into partnership. See yourselves as partners with God and you will experience divine joy and satisfaction.

Bibliography

References related to congregational size dynamics are marked with an asterisk (*).

Caring for the Small Church: Insights From Women in Ministry, by Nancy T. Foltz (Judson Press, 1994). This book highlights areas where the natural gifts of women nurture small-church ministries and vice versa, but it also alludes to the feminine nature of small-church social functioning.

Developing Your Small Church's Potential, by Carl S. Dudley and Douglas Alan Walrath (Judson Press, 1988). Helps congregations understand their role relative to their communities and make use of environmental changes positively.

Dynamics of Small Town Ministry, by Lawrence W. Farris (Alban Institute, 2000). Excellent introduction into the facets of life in a small community and the positive role the church can play.

Entering the World of the Small Church, by Anthony G. Pappas (Alban Institute, 2000). Revised edition explores not only the basic sociological and theological nature of the small church but also harmonious leadership strategies and issues for the future.

*Growing Plans, by Lyle E. Schaller (Abingdon Press, 1983).

Guidelines for Leading Your Congregation: Small Membership Church, by Julia Kuhn Wallace (Cokesbury, 2000).

Help for the Small Church Pastor: Unlocking the Potential of Your Congregation, by Steve R. Bierly (Zondervan, 1995). An easy read, packed with affirmations and practical helps for small-church leaders.

How Your Church Family Works: Understanding Congregations as Emotional Systems, by Peter L. Steinke (Alban Institute, 1993). An easy-to-read text that will shed light on interactive dynamics in small churches.

**The In-Between Church: Navigating Size Transitions in Congregations*, by Alice Mann (Alban Institute, 1998).

Inside the Small Church, edited by Anthony G. Pappas (Alban Institute, 2001). A cornucopia of essays on the rich life of small churches. Readers will come away with a renewed love and appreciation for small churches and new skills for ministry.

The Little Church That Could: Raising Small Church Esteem, by Steven E. Burt and Hazel Ann Roper (Judson Press, 2000). Two major small-church advocates collaborate to do for small churches what society unthinkingly does for large enterprises. Offers examples of on-site application.

Making It Work: Effective Administration in the Small Church, by Douglas A. Walrath (Judson Press, 1994). A positive, practical guide to being a relational administrator.

Making the Small Church Effective, by Carl S. Dudley (Abingdon Press, 1978). The classic that spawned a fresh look at our smaller congregations. A must-read for all serious small-church leaders. A revised edition is scheduled for publication in 2002.

Money, Motivation, and Mission in the Small Church, by Anthony Pappas (Judson Press, 1989). Considers stewardship in the setting of the small church with both optimism and realism. Discusses commonsense budgeting and growing mission efforts.

More Than Numbers: The Ways Churches Grow, by Loren B. Mead (Alban Institute, 1993). A must-read for anyone who thinks numbers are the only measure of congregational success!

Mustard Seeds: Devotions for Small Church People, by Anthony G. Pappas (The Five Stones, 1994). Sixty devotions uplifting the spirit of small-church folk. Each includes a Scripture passage, a meditation, a prayer, and discussion questions. Useful individually, as sermon starters, or in small groups.

Natural Church Development: A Guide to Eight Essential Qualities of Healthy Churches, by Christian A. Schwarz (ChurchSmart Resources, 1996). A fresh look at church health and growth with especially affirmative words for small churches.

The Rural Church: Learning From Three Decades of Change, by Edward W. Hassinger, John S. Holik, and J. Kenneth Benson (Abingdon Press, 1988). Shares characteristics of rural churches and their setting. Reveals an amazing constancy of the total number of rural churches over the three-decade period considered.

Rural Congregational Studies: A Guide for Good Shepherds, by L. Shannon Jung and Mary A. Agria (Abingdon Press, 1997). A manual filled with insights and resources for productive ministry in rural settings.

*Sizing Up a Congregation for New Member Ministry, by Arlin J. Rothauge (The Episcopal Church Center, undated).

Small Churches Can Make a Big Difference video (Discipleship Resources, 1999).

The Small Membership Church: Scenarios for Tomorrow, by Lyle E. Schaller (Abingdon Press, 1994). Posits a positive future for those small churches that are willing to adapt to new roles in society.

Transforming Church Boards Into Communities of Spiritual Leaders, by Charles M. Olsen (Alban Institute, 1995). An invitation to invest the administrative functioning of a congregation with spiritual life. Very appropriate for small congregations.

Vital Ministry in the Small Membership Church. This series of books published by The General Board of Discipleship and Discipleship Resources includes *Biblical Virtues,* by John M. Freeman (1999); *Christian Education,* by Myrtle A. Felkner (2001); *Mission,* by Betty C. Whitehurst (1999); *Sharing Stories, Shaping Community,* by Mike Mather (2002); and *Superintending the Small Church in the 21st Century,* by Deborah K. Cronin (1999).

Welcome! Tools and Techniques for New Member Ministry, by Andrew D. Weeks (Alban Institute, 1992). A practical and comprehensive look at all of the aspects of a church's presentation to the visitor or the unchurched.

Wonderful Worship in Smaller Churches, by David R. Ray (Pilgrim Press, 2000). Filled with principles and illustrations of how worship in family-sized settings can be soul satisfying.